TIME

BY
PAUL BENNETT

THE SANDS OF TIME

This saying comes from the sand clocks (such as hourglasses) that were used to measure short periods of time (such as an hour). The sand trickles through from one half of the clock to the other through a narrow hole. When all of the sand has trickled through, that time is up. The sand clock can be turned over to measure additional time. Another similar saying is "*the sands are running out,*" which means that time is nearly up.

FOR GENERATIONS

This picture shows three generations of a family: children, parents, and grandparents. "Generation" is another way of describing time. A generation is a step in a family tree. It is the time it takes for children to grow up and become parents themselves. Geneologists look back at the history of families from generation to generation.

TIME TICKING AWAY

The White Rabbit from *Alice's Adventures in Wonderland* is famous for taking a watch out of his waistcoat pocket and muttering to himself, "*Oh dear! Oh dear! I shall be too late!*" Just like us, he is very aware of the passing of time. Using watches, we can split up time into tiny bits. Watches can measure seconds – even fractions of seconds – minutes and hours.

OUT WITH THE OLD, IN WITH THE NEW

Old Father Time is seen here carrying the New Year on his shoulders. Time is often represented as an old man, and because the New Year represents new beginnings, it is often depicted as a young child.

REMEMBERING SPECIAL DAYS

Calendars and diaries divide a year up into days, weeks, and months. They also note religious festivals, national holidays, and other special days. Many of these important days happen on the same date each year, and in the case of Halloween it is always on October 31. We also use calendars to remind us of important events in our lives, such as holidays, birthdays, and anniversaries.

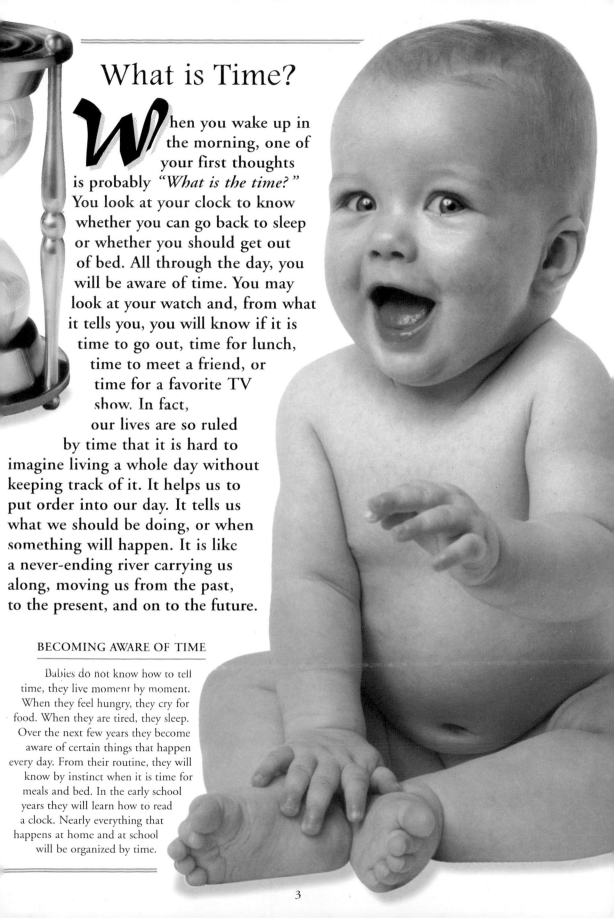

What is Time?

When you wake up in the morning, one of your first thoughts is probably *"What is the time?"* You look at your clock to know whether you can go back to sleep or whether you should get out of bed. All through the day, you will be aware of time. You may look at your watch and, from what it tells you, you will know if it is time to go out, time for lunch, time to meet a friend, or time for a favorite TV show. In fact, our lives are so ruled by time that it is hard to imagine living a whole day without keeping track of it. It helps us to put order into our day. It tells us what we should be doing, or when something will happen. It is like a never-ending river carrying us along, moving us from the past, to the present, and on to the future.

BECOMING AWARE OF TIME

Babies do not know how to tell time, they live moment by moment. When they feel hungry, they cry for food. When they are tired, they sleep. Over the next few years they become aware of certain things that happen every day. From their routine, they will know by instinct when it is time for meals and bed. In the early school years they will learn how to read a clock. Nearly everything that happens at home and at school will be organized by time.

Biological Clocks

NATURAL TIME

Early humans had a very different understanding of time than we do today. They were not aware of seconds, minutes, and hours. They awoke at sunrise and, while it was light, they hunted animals, gathered plants for food, and made tools and shelters. They knew from experience what the creatures would be doing at different times of the day, such as feeding or resting, and which plants would be in fruit. In this way, their circadian rhythm supported their survival, allowing them to fully use the daylight hours.

Before watches and clocks were invented, people were not too concerned with keeping track of time. Their built-in sense of time, a kind of basic rhythm, helped them to live in tune with events in the world around them, such as the rising and falling of the sun and the changing seasons. We also have these basic "clocks" in our bodies today. Scientists have discovered that our pattern of waking and sleeping is following something they call the "circadian rhythm," and this rhythm is affected by the amount of daylight and darkness in our lives. Experiments have shown that people's body clocks are about 25 hours long. Many other living things have their own body clocks. Cold-blooded creatures, such as lizards and snakes, move very slowly early in the morning when they are cold. As they warm themselves in the sun, their body temperature rises and they are able to become active.

MONSTERS OF THE DEEP

Some animals never see sunlight. They live in underground caves or in the deep sea. Although they never see the difference between day and night, they have their own body rhythms that ensure their survival, knowing when to eat, sleep, and mate. This weird-looking fish is a fangtooth and it lives far below the sunlit surface of the seas and oceans.

THE TIDES

The Moon's gravity and, to a lesser extent, that of the Sun cause a rhythmic, twice-daily rising and falling of the tides. Scientists have discovered that the circadian rhythm is very close to the rhythm of the tides – there are two tides every 24 hours and 50 minutes. Some people believe this is because we have evolved from creatures that lived in the primitive oceans millions of years ago – a kind of "ancient memory" that makes our body clocks tick today.

PLANT RHYTHMS

Plants have their own natural rhythms, too. Many flowers open and close according to how much sunlight there is – on a cloudy, dark day some flowers may not open very much at all. Some plants, like sunflowers, also follow the movement of the Sun as it tracks across the sky. They turn their leaves and flowers towards the sunlight, which they need for nourishment and growth in a process called photosynthesis. After pollination, flowers produce seeds which fall to the ground, growing into new plants the following year.

NIGHT SHIFT

The body clocks of many creatures vary even with the same types of animals. For instance, many birds sing during the day, but the owl's hoot is heard at night. Just as the daytime creatures are settling down for the night, the night-time ones are on the move, on the lookout for a tasty meal. Mice, bats, and many insects also wake up when the sun goes down, and their senses are especially adapted to allow them to "see" their dimly lit world just as clearly as we can see ours during the day.

THE MIDNIGHT SUN

Near the North Pole, the sun never sets in summer. There are 24 hours of daylight, and countries such as Greenland (as shown left) that fringe the Arctic Circle are called the "Land of the Midnight Sun." Many people do not adjust well to the long hours of daylight. Their circadian rhythm becomes upset, their sleep suffers, and they feel tired and irritable.

PLANKTON

Even the smallest creatures have body clocks. Plankton are small, drifting animals that live in the oceans. In the daytime they can be found a few hundred feet below the waves where they try to avoid being eaten. As the sun goes down, they move up to the surface of the sea to feed on the plentiful tiny, simple plants, called algae.

The Seasons

From earliest times, people have observed the patterns of the world around them: the regular appearance of the Sun and Moon in the sky; the annual changes in temperature and climate; the growth each year of plants and trees; the movement of animals. From what they saw, they were able to divide up the year into periods with particular weather conditions – spring, summer, autumn, and winter – and to use "nature's clock" to plan for the future. Farmers knew the right time of year to sow seeds or to harvest crops, and also when animals were on their annual migration. Until 500 years ago, no one knew for sure why we have the seasons. It was simply thought to be part of God's great plan, and was not questioned. We now know scientifically that we have the seasons because of the way the Earth rotates around the Sun.

SEASONAL CYCLE IN PLANTS

The changing seasons bring about obvious changes in plants. These changes are triggered by such differences as soil temperature and the length of the day. Perennial plants (those that live for a year or more) have cycles for growing and shedding their leaves. The maple tree is a good example of this. When autumn approaches, nutrients flow back into the tree from the leaves. This changes the leaves from green to yellow to red. When they become brown and dry, they fall off the tree.

HIBERNATION

The biological clocks of many animals are linked to the seasons. An internal "alarm" causes a change in behavior. In the summer and autumn, animals such as bears, hedgehogs, and dormice feed to build up a store of fat which provides the energy they need during hibernation. During their winter sleep, their breathing and heartbeat are slower; they therefore expend very little energy and can survive the harsh winter months without feeding. When the warmer weather arrives, they wake up and return to their summer activities.

THE SOLAR YEAR

This picture shows the Earth's path around the Sun. The Earth's axis is not perfectly upright – it is always tilted slightly. As it moves around the Sun, the Earth rotates and so different parts of the surface of the Earth face the Sun at different times; this makes the seasons. For some months of the year, the North Pole is tilted towards the Sun and the South Pole is tilted away. During this time, the northern hemisphere has the long, warm days of summer while the southern hemisphere has the short, cold days of winter. Later in the year, when the South Pole will be tilted towards the Sun and the North Pole away from it, the seasons in the northern and southern hemisphere are reversed. The solar year is roughly 365¼ days long.

MIGRATION

The spectacular migrations of animals are linked to the seasons and the availability of food. For example, in the African dry season, when there is no rain and all the grass has been eaten, hundreds of thousands of wildebeest sweep across the plains, crossing deep rivers that may be on their way, in order to find new areas where grass is growing. They return when fresh grass springs up again after the rains.

VACATION TIME

Vacations are affected by the seasons as many people take advantage of particular weather conditions. In the cold winter months, sports such as skiing are popular. In the hotter summer months, people flock to beaches or the countryside. Long-distance travel allows people to have a beach vacation in winter.

HARVEST TIME

As summer ends, farmers harvest their crops. Traditionally this was a very important time; for if there was a good harvest, there would be plenty of food to see people through the cold winter months when nothing was growing. It also provided seeds for growing crops in the following spring.

Ancient Timekeeping

THE EGYPTIANS

The earliest Egyptian calendars were based on the movements of the Moon and the annual flooding of the River Nile, which was welcomed as part of the annual cycle of the seasons. Every year the level of the Nile rises dramatically as a result of heavy summer rain falling on mountains to the south. The river overflows its banks and floods the land, leaving a layer of mud that enriches the soil and provides a strip of good farmland in the middle of the desert.

Long before there were clocks, people relied on regular, natural events to keep track of time. They worked, ate, and slept according to the rising and setting of the Sun. Today, we use the word "day" not only to describe the 24 hours from one midnight to the next, but also the period of light from sunrise to sunset. The four seasons, too, were studied, and by keeping track of the Sun's position in the sky, people could mark the passing of one year and the start of another. The quiet winter period, when the farmers prepared the ground for sowing seeds in the coming spring, became the natural end of the year. However, there was no other measure between a day and a year, and so the phases of the Moon were used for further measurements of time.

AZTEC CALENDAR

By observing the natural world, the priests of early farming civilizations were able to make calendars that predicted the seasons. Early calendars, such as this one carved in stone by the Aztec people of Central America, were very elaborate. Archaeologists have discovered that the Sun played an important role in the religious life of many early civilizations, and was worshiped as a god.

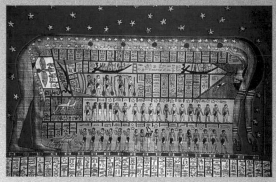

EGYPTIAN SKY GODDESS

Our ancestors formed a cycle of time from observing the natural rhythms of the world around them, which they included in their religion. The people of Ancient Egypt believed that the sky was a goddess called Nut, who arched her body over the Earth, and the Sun was a god called Ra. Every evening Nut swallowed Ra, the setting sun, and every morning she gave birth to him again. Her body was often drawn covered in the stars of the night sky.

SUN WORSHIP

In early times, the sky was believed to be the home of the gods who controlled the movement of the Sun, the changing phases of the Moon, and the seasons. Many cultures worshiped these gods. Astronomer-priests kept records of what they saw and sought ways of honoring the gods by building temples and carrying out rituals. Stonehenge is one of Europe's most important temples. It was built at about 1800 B.C. and was aligned to receive the rays of the midsummer sunrise. Many people believe the astronomer-priests used Stonehenge to predict the motions of the Sun and Moon, and when eclipses might occur.

Breaking Time

THE LUNAR MONTH

Just as the Earth travels around the Sun, the Moon orbits the Earth. Each orbit takes about 29½ days, and is called the lunar month.

This diagram shows the phases of the Moon during each lunar month. With the Sun at the top, and the Earth at the center (blue), the orbit of the Moon is shown twice. The inner ring (red is the far side of the Moon, never seen from Earth) shows the reflection of the Sun's rays on the Moon, while the other half is in shadow. The outer ring shows what the Moon actually looks like from Earth at the different phases. The new Moon is at the top and is not visible in the sky, because the Sun is directly behind it.

The different ways of measuring time – days, months, and years – all worked reasonably well until people tried to put them all together into one calendar. The problem was twofold: the number of days in a lunar month (29½ days) did not fit exactly into a solar year (365¼ days), and the number of lunar months themselves also did not fit into a solar year (12 months 11 days). Everything became very muddled as the calendars became out of step. For example, the early Romans adopted a system of 10 months in a year, which meant that the months that were supposed to come in the winter were falling in the autumn. To solve the problem, they added extra months and days as they needed to. By 46 B.C., the system was in such a mess that the Roman general, Julius Caesar, reformed the calendar. It became known as the Julian calendar and it lasted for the next 1,600 years.

DAYS OF THE WEEK

Seven does not fit exactly into 365 days or 366 days, so why do we have a week made up of seven days? The answer is because the Romans believed seven to be a lucky number. They also saw seven objects in the sky that did not move with the stars: the Sun and the Moon, and the planets Mars, Mercury, Jupiter, Venus, and Saturn. These names, together with names of Norse and Anglo-Saxon gods, have greatly influenced our names for the days of the week.

DAY	ORIGIN OF NAME
Sunday	*Sun*
Monday	*Moon*
Tuesday	*Twi, Norse god of war and the sky*
Wednesday	*Woden, chief Anglo-Saxon god*
Thursday	*Thor, Norse god of thunder (shown here wielding his mighty hammer)*
Friday	*Frigga, Anglo-Saxon goddess of the heavens, and wife of Woden*
Saturday	*Saturn, Roman god of agriculture*

EARTH-CENTERED UNIVERSE

For thousands of years, astronomers believed that the Earth was the center of the universe and that the Sun, Moon, planets, and a huge sphere to which the stars were fixed, all circled the Earth. This became known as the Ptolemaic system after the Greek astronomer, Ptolemy, whose theories of an Earth-centered universe were to rule the world of astronomy for 1,500 years.

NICOLAUS COPERNICUS

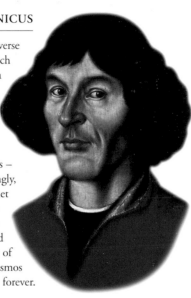

The idea of an Earth-centered universe was supported by the Church, which believed that God had created a universe with the Earth at its heart. Then in 1543, the Polish astronomer, Nicolaus Copernicus, published a book that said that the Sun was at the center of the system of planets and stars – not the Earth. Not surprisingly, Copernicus's ideas were met with great hostility by the Church, but he changed our view of the cosmos forever.

THE JULIAN CALENDAR

Julius Caesar's reforms removed the muddle surrounding the calendar. Instead of 10 months in a year, he introduced a year made up of 12 unequal months, seven of them having 31 days, four 30 days, and one 28 days (making 365 days in total). But because a solar year does not add up to an exact number of days, every fourth year had an extra day added. This became known as a leap year. This system abandoned any connection with the phases of the Moon, although the religious festivals of Easter for Christians and Ramadan for Muslims are still worked out using lunar months.

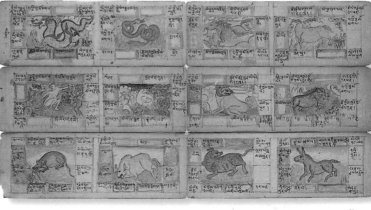

THE CHINESE CALENDAR

The Chinese year is measured by the Sun, while the months are reckoned by the Moon. An extra month is added at regular intervals to keep the two systems of measurement in line. The Chinese name each year after an animal. There are 12 animals in all, their year being repeated as part of a regular cycle. Each cycle starts with the Year of the Rat, followed by the Years of the Ox, Tiger, Rabbit, Dragon, Snake, Horse, Ram, Monkey, Cock, Dog, and Pig. Much like the zodiac, each animal is associated with particular personality characteristics, so people born in the Year of the Rabbit, for example, will be happy and content and blessed with a large family.

Today's Dates

THE MODERN CALENDAR

The calendar we use today is the Gregorian calendar, named after the Pope who introduced it in 1582. To correct the "missing" 10 days Pope Gregory XIII ordered that the day after October 4 would be October 15. But this did not solve the whole problem because a new error would slowly build up and another 10 days would be lost again in 1,600 years' time. His solution was to have three fewer days every 400 years. A leap year adds on an extra day, so his calendar would have three fewer leap years every 400 years. Thus the years 1700, 1800, and 1900 were not leap years but the year 2000 is. His calendar is not perfect, however. In about 3,000 years' time, there will be another "missing" day.

Today, all the countries of the world use the Gregorian calendar for official purposes.

The Julian calendar was a great success and overcame all the problems of having a calendar that did not match the solar year. Or so everyone thought. In fact, the solar year is not exactly 365¼ days, but is shorter by 11 minutes 14 seconds. This seems to be a tiny amount of time to deal with when compared to a whole year. But over a period of 128 years it resulted in the loss of a day. By the year 1580, more than 1,600 years after the Julian calendar had been introduced, the calendar was wrong by 10 days. Pope Gregory XIII was greatly concerned about this for it was becoming difficult to calculate the date of Easter, which was drifting very slowly back towards Christmas. He therefore consulted his astronomers who were able to calculate the actual length of the solar year, which forms the basis of our modern calendar, known as the Gregorian calendar.

WHAT IS THE YEAR?

The Gregorian calendar had been calculated from when Christians believe Christ was born. The years before Christ's birth are B.C. (before Christ) and the years after are A.D. (*Anno Domini*, Latin for "year of our Lord"). The Jewish religious calendar dates from when Jews believe the world was created, and the Muslim calendar from when Muhammad moved to Medina. In recognition of the different traditions, the letters B.C.E. (before the common era) and C.E. (common era) are sometimes used instead of the Christian B.C. and A.D.

GEORGE WASHINGTON'S BIRTHDAY

First not everyone accepted the new Gregorian calendar – it was used mostly by countries that followed the Catholic religion. When George Washington, the first President of the United States (1732-99), was born, the American colonies followed the Protestant religion and still used the Julian calendar. His birthday then was February 11. According to our current Gregorian calendar, taking into account the missing days, George Washington's birthday is February 22.

CHINESE NEW YEAR

All around the world, the New Year officially begins on January 1. But in many countries there are calendars that are still based on the Moon. For example, the Chinese New Year begins on the first day of a lunar year, some time between January 21 and February 19. It is marked with colorful processions, fireworks, and presents.

HINDU FESTIVALS

These festivals follow the phases of the Moon, so the dates of the festivals change from year to year. This girl is celebrating Diwali, the Hindu festival of lights. Diwali falls in the autumn months of October or November. Small lamps are lit every night of the four day celebrations. The lamps are symbols of the power of goodness over the forces of darkness.

THE MUSLIM YEAR

The Muslim calendar is based on the position and movement of the Moon. There are 12 calendar months, which are either 29 or 30 days long, making the Islamic year shorter than a Christian year. Unlike the Christian day, which is from midnight to midnight, the Muslim day starts and ends at sunset. This ancient picture shows a procession at the end of the Muslim festival of Ramadan, which lasts for one lunar month.

THE JEWISH CALENDAR

The Jewish calendar is based on the movements of the Moon. Because of this, the dates of the months in the Jewish religion vary from year to year. The month of the Jewish New Year occurs in September or October and the festival of Passover, which is being celebrated here, falls in March or April. There are 12 calendar months, but an extra month is added in a Jewish leap year.

Timekeeping: Using the Elements

The Ancient Egyptians were the first people to divide a whole day into 24 hours. They divided up the night into 12 parts according to the regular movement of the stars across the heavens. As a particular star rose into the night sky, they knew an hour had passed and a new one was about to start. They decided to divide up the day into 12 equal parts, too, but during the hours of daylight the stars could not be seen. To solve the problem they used the movement of the Sun and the shadow that a sundial casts to keep track of time. Later, the hours were divided up into smaller and smaller units – into minutes and seconds, with 60 seconds in a minute and 60 minutes in an hour.

The Babylonians are believed to be the first civilization to count using 60 as a base for working out large numbers; therefore, the way we divide up hours into minutes and minutes into seconds may have been influenced by them.

CHINESE WATER CLOCK

This Chinese clepsydra has containers set at different levels so that it forms a kind of staircase down which the water flows. When all the water reaches the bottom, the timekeeper records the time and carries the water up the ladder to the highest container to start the process all over again.

SHIP'S BELL

In the past, a bell was rung on board ships to signal half-hour intervals. At sea, the day was broken up into six four-hour periods called watches, and a member of the crew had to ring the bell while on duty.

TIME TRICKLING AWAY

The clepsydra is a clock that uses water to measure the time. The Egyptians used clepsydras over 2,500 years ago. They were water-filled vessels with a hole in the base through which the water drained away. Some were marked with lines relating to the 12 hours of the night. There were many different designs of clepsydra. The one on the right is from southern India. A bowl with a small hole in its base was placed in a large dish of water. The bowl filled gradually over time, and when it was full the attendant beat a gong.

CLEPSYDRA, SOUTHERN INDIA

CANDLE CLOCK

For many centuries candle clocks were used to keep track of time. It is said that they were invented by the English king, Alfred the Great, in the 9th century. Whether or not he was the true inventor, the candle clock was an important way of keeping track of time. The candle was often divided up into sections, each of which took an hour to burn down.

SUNDIALS

On a sundial there is a pointer, called a gnomon, which casts a shadow onto a flat base. The base is marked with a scale to show the hours of the day. As the position of the Sun in the sky changes, the shadow from the gnomon changes direction, too, and the time can be seen on the scale. This sundial is from the Forbidden City in China.

SEASONS & SHADOWS

Shadows cast by the Sun change length as well as direction. The shadows are longest in the morning and evening when the Sun is low on the horizon, and shortest at midday when the Sun is overhead. The seasons, as well as time, can be determined from the length of the shadow. In summer, the Sun is higher in the sky than in winter. These tribesmen in Borneo are measuring the length of a shadow cast from a stick planted in the ground. By always measuring the shadow at midday, they can tell how the seasons are changing.

GRAND CLOCKS

Large, public clocks, such as this one in St. Mark's Square, in Venice, Italy (left), are often very ornate. On the clock face (right) the 24 hours of the day are marked in Roman numerals in the outer ring. Inside the hours are the signs of the zodiac, representing the months or time of the year. Bells ring to let everyone know the time of the day, even if they cannot see the clock.

GRANDFATHER CLOCK

This ornate grandfather clock was made in France in the 18th century. A grandfather clock has a falling weight which provides the energy to keep the pendulum swinging inside the clock. The weight is attached to a long chain so that the clock works for several days before it stops.

THE H1

This odd-looking clock is the invention of the English clockmaker, John Harrison. It was his attempt to win a £20,000 cash prize offered by the British Government to anyone who could solve the problem of fixing a ship's position at sea. Many people thought the study of the stars was a key, but Harrison proved that the solution lay in accurate timekeeping. The rolling of the ship made pendulum clocks unworkable. Harrison's clock, called the H1, had a new mechanism and separate dials for seconds, minutes, hours, and the days of the month. Although the clock proved to work very well, Harrison wanted to make a clock that was smaller and even more accurate (see page 22).

Timekeeping: The Mechanical Clock

Until about 600 years ago, sundials were the most popular way of measuring time. There were mechanical clocks, but they had bells instead of hands to tell the time, and they were not very accurate. The word "clock" probably comes from *clocca*, the Latin word for bell. Then, in the 1650s, there was a great breakthrough in clock making when a Dutch scientist, Christiaan Huygens, built the first pendulum clock. A pendulum is a weight swinging from a fixed point. He realized that the regular swing of the pendulum would be perfect for measuring time accurately. All mechanical clocks need a way of moving the hands at an even speed, and Huygens found a way of linking the pendulum's swing to a mechanism that would move the hands in regular ticks.

GALILEO'S DISCOVERY

In the 1580s, the Italian mathematician and astronomer, Galileo, discovered how the pendulum worked. While sitting in Pisa Cathedral he watched the swing of a hanging lamp as it moved to and fro. He measured the time it took to make a complete swing and discovered that it took the same amount of time to get back to where it started, even when the size of the swing changed. Galileo applied this observation to experiments with a pendulum, but he never made a pendulum clock.

CHRISTIAAN HUYGENS

This Dutch scientist revolutionized timekeeping when he built the first pendulum clock. The arc of the pendulum's swing gets smaller and smaller until it eventually stops. To keep the pendulum swinging, he attached a small weight to a reel. As the weight falls very gradually, it pulls the reel around and this keeps the pendulum swinging. Each week the weight is lifted with a winding key.

KEEPING TIME

Musicians use a metronome to keep time with the beat of the music. The metronome indicates the tempo or speed of music by producing a clicking sound from a swinging arm (the pendulum). A small weight on the arm controls the speed of the swing, which can be adjusted by the musician.

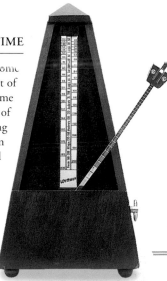

BIG BEN

Big Ben is the name of the great bell in the clock tower of the Houses of Parliament in London. A clock with a 13-foot pendulum, it is famed for its accuracy. Big Ben first boomed out in 1859.

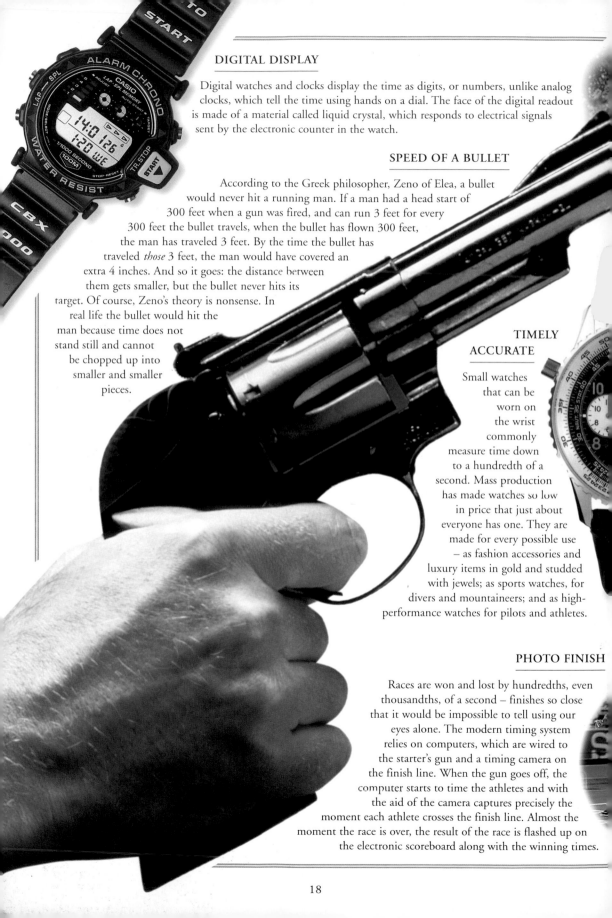

DIGITAL DISPLAY

Digital watches and clocks display the time as digits, or numbers, unlike analog clocks, which tell the time using hands on a dial. The face of the digital readout is made of a material called liquid crystal, which responds to electrical signals sent by the electronic counter in the watch.

SPEED OF A BULLET

According to the Greek philosopher, Zeno of Elea, a bullet would never hit a running man. If a man had a head start of 300 feet when a gun was fired, and can run 3 feet for every 300 feet the bullet travels, when the bullet has flown 300 feet, the man has traveled 3 feet. By the time the bullet has traveled *those* 3 feet, the man would have covered an extra 4 inches. And so it goes: the distance between them gets smaller, but the bullet never hits its target. Of course, Zeno's theory is nonsense. In real life the bullet would hit the man because time does not stand still and cannot be chopped up into smaller and smaller pieces.

TIMELY ACCURATE

Small watches that can be worn on the wrist commonly measure time down to a hundredth of a second. Mass production has made watches so low in price that just about everyone has one. They are made for every possible use – as fashion accessories and luxury items in gold and studded with jewels; as sports watches, for divers and mountaineers; and as high-performance watches for pilots and athletes.

PHOTO FINISH

Races are won and lost by hundredths, even thousandths, of a second – finishes so close that it would be impossible to tell using our eyes alone. The modern timing system relies on computers, which are wired to the starter's gun and a timing camera on the finish line. When the gun goes off, the computer starts to time the athletes and with the aid of the camera captures precisely the moment each athlete crosses the finish line. Almost the moment the race is over, the result of the race is flashed up on the electronic scoreboard along with the winning times.

Timekeeping: In Today's World

Bang! Today we have the means to reduce time to such a fine degree that we can photograph a bullet as it is shot from a gun. High-speed photography is just one of the benefits that have come from modern methods of keeping time. The incredibly tiny fractions of a second that can be measured have helped scientists understand more about our world and the nature of the universe. In our everyday lives, we use watches that people just 40 years ago would have been amazed to see. The revolution in the way we keep and use time has been led by the development of the quartz watch in the late 1960s. Quartz is a common mineral found in the ground. When a small current of electricity from a battery is passed through the quartz, it vibrates an exact number of times a second. Microchips, like the ones found in computers, count the vibrations and display the time on the watch face.

SPRING DRIVEN

In the mechanical watch, the pendulum and weight of the bulky grandfather clock have been replaced by tiny coiled springs, which drive the mechanism and regulate the speed of the wheels which drive the hands.

The modern spring-driven watch is one of the most precise mechanical things ever made.

ATOMIC CLOCKS

These clocks are so incredibly accurate that they lose or gain no more than a second once every two or three million years! Atomic clocks use the energy changes that take place in atoms to keep track of time. This example is the US NBS-4 atomic clock with its keeper.

Timetables

Throughout the day, we check our watches to see that we are on time for the next thing we have to do. In our minds we have a list or table of events that must be done that day, and, as the seconds, minutes, and hours tick past, we move from one thing to the next. Often our busy schedules are set by others: teachers at school must know when their lessons start and finish, public transportation needs to run on time, and the times of TV shows are published well in advance. Nothing we do, it seems, happens without reference to some sort of timetable. The need for timetables started in the 19th century when the first big factories were built and it became important for people to work together under one roof. People no longer worked according to the season and the natural rhythms of the day. Now our lives are organized so that everyone turns up and leaves the school, factory, or office at the right time, all year round.

TV TIMES

TV and radio guides are also timetables. They are published in newspapers and magazines, and are arranged so that you can see the times of the programs at a glance and so plan your night's viewing with ease. You can set a video recorder to record a program at a particular time.

CALL TO PRAYER

Even in our time-conscious world we do not always rely on clocks and watches to tell us to do things. Muslims are called to prayer by an official, or muezzin, from the minaret of the mosque where they worship. In Christian countries, some churches ring bells on Sundays, at weddings, and other important days. In Israel, a siren heralds the start of the Jewish sabbath, which begins on Friday at sunset.

SHEPHERD PATENTEE
53 LF HALL LONDON
GALVANO-MAGNETIC CLOCK

GOOD TIMING

We can use time to make life easier. For example, our busy roads would be brought to a standstill without traffic lights. At busy intersections, traffic from one direction is allowed time to clear before cars from another direction are allowed to cross. The timing of the traffic lights is set so that no one is kept waiting too long and can be varied according to the time of the day.

CLOCKING IN

Are you a slave to time? Time has become so important to us that it is even used to keep track of people. Factories have always had methods of "clocking in and out" – workers register the time they arrive and leave the factory by putting a card into a machine attached to a clock. The machine stamps the time on the card.

MAKING CONNECTIONS

Timetables are vital for planning journeys. Not only do they tell you when buses, trains, or airplanes depart, they also help you to make the connection between different stages of the journey. Timetables became important in the 19th century and were widely used by the newly formed railroad companies to advertise their services. By knowing when the trains would run, passengers could plan their journey well in advance.

TWENTY-FOUR-HOUR CLOCK

To avoid confusion, timetables are arranged using the 24-hour system of time. We divide the day into two lots of 12 hours and put A.M. (short for the Latin *ante meridiem*, which means "before noon") or P.M. (*post meridiem*, which means "after noon") after the time to tell us if the time is morning or afternoon; for example, 6 A.M. and 6 P.M. This clock shows the time as a 24-hour period, where A.M. and P.M. are not used. Instead of the day being split into two, the hours continue past 12 to 24. Therefore 06:00 is 6 A.M., and 18:00 is 6 P.M.

WINDING DOWN

In a clock, when the coiled spring that provides the power to make it work becomes slack, the clock slows down and eventually stops. This is called "winding down." To make the clock work again, the spring must be tightened or wound up. Similarly, we use the phrase "winding down" when we forget our busy timetable and begin to relax. And we often say we are "wound up" when we feel tense or anxious.

Keeping the World on Time

As the Earth spins, some parts of the world are in sunlight while others are in darkness. For example, when it is noon in New York in the U.S., it is midnight in Perth, Australia. It is impossible to set the same time for every part of the world, so each area has its own local time according to when the Sun rises and sets. To reflect this, the world has been divided up into time zones, bands on the Earth's surface with the same time. There are 24 time zones, reflecting the 24 hours of the day. As the Earth turns through a complete circle of 360 degrees in a day, each time zone covers 15 degrees. The *Bureau International de l'Heure* in Paris coordinates the world's time signals, or Coordinated Universal Time (UTC). It uses atomic clocks to send out signals accurate to a millisecond.

THE PRIME MERIDIAN

Since 1884, the world has measured its time from the Prime Meridian which runs through Greenwich in London. A meridian is an imaginary line of longitude that runs from Pole to Pole. Greenwich is set at 0 degrees longitude, and the local time at Greenwich is known as Greenwich Mean Time (GMT) or Universal Time (UT). As you move west and cross 15 degrees of longitude, you move into a new time zone and must put your watch back by an hour. Conversely, as you move east, you must put your watch forward.

JOHN HARRISON & H4

John Harrison (1693–1776), the inventor of the H1 (see page 16), pursued his quest to win a prize awarded to the inventor of a clock that found longitude to within half of a degree (equal to two minutes of time). This meant it could not lose or gain more than three seconds in 24 hours. Harrison's H4 watch (left) was tested on a voyage to the West Indies in 1761–62. It lost only five seconds during the journey, which meant the navigator could work out where he was on a map with an accuracy of about a half mile.

GLOBAL POSITIONING SYSTEM (GPS)

Modern methods of finding longitude and latitude have changed navigational methods greatly. Satellite navigation, or NAVSAT, has helped ships' crews and airline pilots for over 20 years. With a GPS device (right), which is about the same size as a mobile phone, sailors can find both their position and direction, or heading, anywhere in the world to less than 1/16 of a mile.

THE AGE OF SAIL

The old sailing ships navigated with the aid of accurate clocks called chronometers. Out in the open ocean there were no landmarks to give them their position. But by having an accurate clock set to GMT, sailors could find how far east or west they were (their longitude) from the Prime Meridian. To discover their latitude – how far north or south they were – they took the angle of the Sun during the day or certain stars at night. They drew their lines of latitude and longitude on a map; where the two lines met was their position on the ocean. This old globe is marked with the lines of longitude and latitude.

NAVSTAR

NAVSTAR (navigation system using time and ranging) is the satellite system at the heart of satellite navigation technology. As the satellites orbit the Earth, they send out signals that can be picked up by a GPS device (above).

TIME ZONES OF THE WORLD

Long plane journeys often result in jet lag – a general feeling of physical and mental tiredness. This is because our natural body clocks have become out of step with the time zone we are in. Planes often travel over several time zones in a short period of time. The time difference between England and New York is five hours, the journey is approximately seven hours. So, if you took off from London at lunchtime, when you arrived in New York the time there would only be two hours later; however your body clock would tell you it was evening. It takes your body clock a few days to adjust to the new time zone, which is why you often feel tired for a couple of days after a flight.

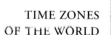

| -12 | -11 | -10 | -9 | -8 | -7 | -6 | -5 | -4 | -3 | -2 | -1 | 0 | +1 | +2 | +3 | +4 | +5 | +6 | +7 | +8 | +9 | +10 | +11 | +12 |

INTERNATIONAL DATE LINE

NORTH AMERICA

GREENWICH

EUROPE

ASIA

AFRICA

SOUTH AMERICA

AUSTRALIA

INTERNATIONAL DATE LINE

Looking Back in Time

THE COMPUTER AGE

Periods in history that are marked by some important feature are often given a special name, such as "the computer age." We now take personal computers for granted but just 40 years ago they existed only in people's fantasies. Computers are now used everywhere – in our homes, in industry, in hospitals – which is why the "millennium bug" is seen as a potential disaster. Many computers need their internal clocks reset to recognize the date 2000 – the millennium year.

When we look back in time, we see the days, months, and years going back into the past in a neat sequence, or chronological order. Events have their place in history, and we can use time lines to show where these events fit into the chronological order – when they occurred and how long they went on for. By placing events in history, we can also assess their significance and the effects they have had. This is important to us as it helps us to make sense of the changes and the direction we are going in the future. History gives meaning to our lives and can also give us a sense of identity. We divide up the past in many different ways according to the changes. Records are important for this. The evidence of the past is all around us: written documents, paintings and photographs, buildings, historical artifacts – or just our own memories.

1903
The first powered flight of the Wright brothers

1912
Sinking of the Titanic

1914
Start of the First World War

NATURAL LOG-BOOKS

Trees are the longest-living things on the Earth. Every year they develop a growth ring, which represents one year on a time line. Cross-sections of very old trees have hundreds of growth rings. If you know when the tree was cut down, you can link its rings with great events in history. When the weather is dry, trees do not grow very much and so the growth ring is narrow. When the weather encourages growth, the ring is wide. Scientists have used this information to discover what the climate was like, even in ancient times.

CHANGING FASHIONS

We often date things according to what was in fashion over a set period, such as a decade. For example, people think of the 1960s as "the swinging sixties": skirts got shorter, hair got longer, the music of groups, such as the Beatles, was a driving force in society, and many long-held beliefs went through radical change.

WARS AND REVOLUTIONS

Wars have a dramatic effect on the lives of people, so when people look back in history they may refer to a war to describe a particular period. Historians often divide up the 20th century into the years of the First World War (1914–18) and the Second World War (1939–45) and the periods before, between, and after them. Revolutions are times of great change within a country, so these, too, are often used to mark different periods of history. For example, the Russian Revolution (1917) saw the establishment of a communist government in Russia. The Industrial Revolution (1750–1850) changed Britain from a rural society to an industrial society.

TIME GONE BY

We all remember what it was like when we were younger – the toys we had, the games we played, our time at school. But these same experiences differ in each generation, and the memories of an elderly person will be entirely different from someone just 20 or 30 years younger.

KINGS AND QUEENS

Historians often speak of the past in terms of the reigns of kings and queens, or the terms of presidents and governments. For example, "Elizabethan" is a term used to describe the period when Elizabeth I was Queen of England (1558–1603). Her reign was notable for commercial growth and a flourishing of the arts. Other examples are the "Reagan years," the period when Ronald Reagan was President of the United States, and "Thatcherism," a phrase coined when Margaret Thatcher was Prime Minister in Great Britain.

LIFE SPAN

A life span is a period of time when living things or machines may be expected to live or work. Every living thing has its own life span. People have a life span of approximately 75 years, some tortoises may live for 150 years, but trees can live for many centuries, even millennia.

Geological Time

Humans have only been on Earth for a comparatively short period of time. If the history of the world is compared to a 24-hour period, humans would only appear in the last few seconds before midnight. So how are scientists able to tell how the Earth was formed hundreds of millions of years before people existed? One way is to date rocks by measuring the small amounts of radioactivity in them. When the rocks were formed, radioactive elements were trapped inside. These elements slowly give out energy at a known rate, enabling scientists to calculate the date of the formation of the rocks. The timescale that shows the important events in the Earth's history is called the geological record.

ICE AGES

There is dramatic evidence for the Ice Ages of the past – landscapes with deep, u-shaped and steep-sided valleys, such as in the Alps in Europe. The great weight of huge rivers of ice, hundreds of feet thick, pressed down on the valley floor. Rocks and boulders trapped in the ice acted like sandpaper as the ice pushed forward, forming the typical features we see today.

GRAND CANYON

The Colorado River in the United States has cut deeply into the land, forming a deep gorge known as the Grand Canyon. The layers of rock you see in the picture were once moving sand and mud on the bottom of a sea. Over millions of years, they dried and hardened into mudstone and sandstone many feet thick.

EVOLUTIONARY TIME

Geologists think the Earth is 4,550 million years old and the earliest forms of life appeared 3,500 million years ago. There is evidence that modern humans, people like ourselves, lived in Africa around 100,000 years ago. However, establishing the theory of how we evolved from the apes is difficult because of the scattered evidence of fossilized remains.

RADIOCARBON DATING

Carbon is the basis of life – it is found in every tissue of all the animals and plants that ever lived. Scientists have discovered that one particular form of carbon, called carbon 14, is only absorbed by a living thing while it is still alive. Carbon 14 gives off tiny amounts of radioactivity, and when something dies, this radioactivity gets weaker and weaker in a process called radioactive decay. By discovering how weak this decay has become, scientists can see how long ago the thing lived. This piece of reindeer bone is being prepared for radiocarbon dating.

BRISTLECONE PINE

This tree, which grows on the slopes of the Rocky Mountains in the United States, is among the oldest-living trees in the world. Some bristlecone pines are up to 5,000 years old, and were seedlings before the pyramids were built in Egypt.

THE FOSSIL RECORD

Fossils are the dead remains of animals and plants that have been embedded in rock and preserved for hundreds of millions of years. By studying fossils, geologists are able to work out what early creatures, such as dinosaurs, looked like, and by dating the rock, discover when they lived. Prehistoric time is divided into stages called eras, and subdivided into periods. Scientists can date these periods according to the age of the fossils they find.

Space Time

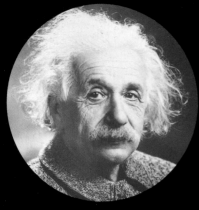

ALBERT EINSTEIN (1879–1955)

In 1905, this great thinker came up with totally different ways of explaining how the universe worked. These ideas were included in his theory of special relativity, and it showed that strange things happen when things move at very high speeds. For example, moving clocks run slower than clocks that are standing still. In 1916, he also came up with a description of how the universe works in his general theory of relativity. This was a theory of gravity, and it predicted an expanding universe.

On Earth, a mile is a good way of measuring long distances, but in space the huge gulfs between the stars is so great that it becomes meaningless. We have to use another way of measuring distances in the universe that is more manageable. So scientists have come up with a clever way of measuring the sheer vastness between the stars and it involves time – the light year. Light travels incredibly fast – at about 186,000 miles a second – which is about 5.88 trillion (a trillion is one million, million) miles a year. This is a very, very long way; but in the emptiness of space, a light year is still a relatively short distance. For example, the Earth is part of the Milky Way, a spiral galaxy which is about 1,500 light years thick at the center and 150,000 light years across. Beyond the Milky Way there are countless more galaxies even larger than our own!

ABSOLUTE TIME

Isaac Newton (1642–1727) thought that time flowed at the same rate for everyone, no matter where they were. He called this "absolute time," and believed that everyone and everything must be at the same moment of "now" throughout the universe. Newton also discovered rules, or laws, on which the universe runs. They explained for the first time how the planets and stars move. He saw the universe as a giant clockwork machine, with everything running along lines that could be worked out in advance. Newton's ideas were unchallenged for 200 years.

THE BEGINNING
OF TIME

The Big Bang is one theory
that explains the origins
of the universe. This
says that all the stuff
of the universe was
once held in a
single, incredibly
dense state.
But then, in
a cataclysmic
explosion, all
the matter was
hurled out in
all directions
forming the
galaxies, stars,
and planets
we see today.
By studying the
rate of expansion
of the universe,
astronomers believe
the Big Bang took place
about 12 billion years ago.

TIME ON JUPITER

If we lived on Jupiter, our days
and years would be very
different. Jupiter is the
giant planet of the solar
system – its bulk, or
mass, is over 300 times
that of the Earth. Despite
its size, it spins very fast,
making a day just 10
hours long. And, whereas
the Earth takes a year to go
around the sun, Jupiter takes
12 years. The length of a day
and a year are different for all
the planets of the solar system.

INTO THE PAST

The spectacular Eagle
Nebula is a cloud of
particles and gases
7,000 light years
away from Earth.
This means that we
see it as it was 7,000
years ago, since this is
the time it took for
the light to reach the
Earth. Whenever we
look up at the night
sky, we are really
looking back into
the past. We do not
really know what is happening right now in the huge vastness of
space simply because the light has not yet reached us!

The Fourth Dimension

What is time? Where does time go? Time appears to go at different speeds according to what you are doing. If you are bored, time seems to drag; if you are enjoying yourself, time seems to fly. Time is very "slippery" since it cannot be pinned down or held like an object – but it always goes in one direction, like an arrow pointing from the past into the future. But what if time was not like that? What if the time that you use was not lost forever? Or you could jump backwards and forwards through time? It would be very strange if time suddenly reversed itself – clocks would run backwards, people would grow young again, and birds would fly backwards! Thinking of time as a "fourth dimension" is the stuff of science fiction, but is it all make-believe? Only time will tell.

DEFYING TIME

Will it ever be possible to defy time? For a young person never to grow old? Knowledge of the secrets of eternal youth have been claimed by many people since ancient times. Creams, cosmetics, diets – even surgery – promise to make us look younger, but, like all past methods, they will not stop us from dying of old age. Scientists are beginning to unlock the secrets of the aging process and may discover a way to live longer – but not forever. Some people think that future technology will allow them to live longer and they choose to be frozen when they die, in a technique called "cryogenics." More bizarre is the story of Jeremy Bentham (above) who, in 1832, willed his body to medical science on the condition that his skeleton be dressed in his own clothes with a wax likeness of his face. He still sits, greeting visitors, at Universty College in London.

CHANGING HISTORY

Traveling back into the past seems like a wonderful idea. You could warn the captain of the *Titanic* that he should change course to avoid the iceberg that will sink his ship. But changing that piece of history means that hundreds of passengers would have lived who in fact died, changing family trees forever. Perhaps this would have led to you never being born, then how could you have warned the captain? Nothing is straightforward when considering time as the Fourth Dimension.

THE FOURTH DIMENSION

We often hear about time as the fourth dimension, which can be added to the three dimensions of space that give form and shape: height, width, and depth. It's as if time and space are two different things – space is the expanse in which we move around, whereas time is something we move with or through. However, according to Einstein, space and time are not separate, but joined together in a single entity called space-time. They only exist together and you could not have one without the other.

TIME TRAVEL

Films such as *Back to the Future* and *Bill and Ted's Excellent Adventure* play around with the idea of time travel, but is time travel possible? Scientists believe that black holes could be the key – fall through one and you might end up in another time and place. Black holes are stars that have collapsed in on themselves and the gravity is so strong that not even light can escape. However, the theory goes that the universe you end up in might not be the one you started from. Indeed, there may be many different universes all linked together by lots of different black holes.

DID YOU KNOW?

That when the Gregorian calendar was introduced into Britain in 1752 there were riots in the streets? When the government finally decided to adopt Pope Gregory XIII's calendar, thus solving the error of a missing day every 128 years under the Julian calendar, special announcements and arrangements were made to make the adjustment go smoothly. This was done by following September 2 with September 14, making a total loss of 11 days. However, ordinary people thought their lives had been shortened and days of wages had been lost, so they rioted, shouting, "Give us back our 11 days!"

That scientists used atomic clocks to prove that moving clocks run slower than stationary clocks? Atomic clocks were used in the experiment because they are so incredibly accurate. One clock was flown around the world and its time was compared with the clock that was left on the ground. The difference was measured in billionths of a second, but it was enough to prove that time slows down as predicted by Einstein's theory of special relativity.

That the man who revolutionized our ideas of time and space, Albert Einstein, would get so involved in his thought experiments that he would lose all track of time? Rather than making scientific discoveries by carrying out practical experiments, Einstein worked out all of his theories about time and space in his head. Often he would leave home for a walk and he would be so caught up in his imagination that he would wander for hours totally unaware of what time it was!

That at Greenwich on the River Thames in England, sailors set their clocks by a falling ball? Long before satellite navigation, sailors navigated with the help of time: by knowing the exact time at Greenwich (on the Prime Meridian) they could work out their longitude at sea. So to help sailors set their clocks to the time at Greenwich, a red ball that was at the top of a tall mast was lowered at exactly 1 P.M. This could be seen from any nearby ship.

That astronomers have predicted that time and space may end with the big crunch? Millions of years from now, the universe may stop expanding and begin to collapse. The galaxies would shrink and form black holes. At the final moment, all the black holes would merge, sucking all the last matter of the universe into one large black hole, destroying time and space. Possibly a new big bang may follow the big crunch, creating a new cycle of Creation.

There's no right answer to the question "What exactly is time?" As you have read, time can be seen in lots of different ways. If you ask a farmer, he would talk about the seasons; if you ask a businessman, he might say that "time is money"; and if you ask a historian, she might tell you about the past. The answer will reflect what is important to that person or what they are doing at the time. Perhaps that is why there are so many odd sayings about time. For example, you might hear someone say, "Time on my hands weighs heavy." Have you ever held time in your hands or placed it on the scales to weigh how heavy it is? A watch or clock maybe, but they only tell the time – they are not time itself. Whatever that is!

ACKNOWLEDGMENTS

We would like to thank: Graham Rich, Rosalind Beckman, and Elizabeth Wiggans for their assistance.
First edition for the United States, Canada, and the Philippines published by Barron's Educational Series, Inc., 1999
First published in Great Britain in 1999 by *ticktock* Publishing Ltd., The Office, The Square, Hadlow, Kent, TN11 0DD, United Kingdom
Copyright © 1999 ticktock Publishing Ltd. American edition Copyright © 1999 Barron's Educational Series, Inc.
All rights reserved. No part of this book may be reproduced in any form, by photostat, microfilm, xerography, or any other means, or incorporated into any information retrieval system, electronic or mechanical, without the written permission of the copyright owner.
All inquiries should be addressed to: Barron's Educational Series, Inc. • 250 Wireless Boulevard • Hauppauge, New York 11788 • http://www.barronseduc.com
Library of Congress Catalog Card No. 98-74958
International Standard Book Number 0-7641-0643-0
Picture research by Image Select. Printed in Hong Kong.
987654321

Picture Credits: t=top, b=bottom, c=center, l=left, r=right, OFC=outside front cover, OBC=outside back cover, IFC=inside front cover
AKG Photo: 8/9ct, 13tr, 13r, 16tr, 16c, 17tr. All Sports Photo/Mike Powell: 18/19b. Ann Ronan@Image Select: 2c, 2bl, 11br, 11tr, 15bl, 16/17c, 21cr, 28bl. Ann Ronan Picture Library: 6/7t, 8tl, 10/11b. Bridgemann Art Library: 10/11t, 11c. Breitling: 18/19c & OFC. Colorific: 10bl, 20bl, 31c. CFCL@Image Select: 13c, 17cb, 18tl, 26tl. e.t. archive: 7br. FPG International: 26c. Image Select: 9tr. J. Allan Cash Ltd: 4/5t & OFC, 12/13t & OBC, 14bl. John Frost: 24/25t. Jean Loup Charmet: 14cr. Mary Evans Picture Library: 12bl, 14tl, 15tr, 22br. National Maritime Museum Library: 16bl & OBC, 20/21b, 22bl, 22tl. National Portrait Gallery, London: 25r. Natural History Museum, London: 4tl. Planet Earth Pictures: 4bl & OBC, 5cb, 24bl, 25br, 27tr, 28bl, 28/29b, 29br. PIX S.A.: 5tr, 6cb & OFC, OFC (Stonehenge). Popperfoto: 25tr & OBC. Rex Features, London: 21c, 23tr, 24/25b. Science Photo Library: 4/5b, 10tl, 19br & OFC, 26b, 26/27t, 28tl, 28/29t, 29b, 30/31t & IFC, 30/31(main pic). Sony: 20tl. Telegraph Colour Picture Library UK: 2/3t & OFC, 3br, 4bl, 5cr, 6/7c, 7r, 8/9 (main pic), 12tl, 14/15c & OFC & 32c, 17br, 18/19t, 19r, 21cb, 23c, 24tl. The Kobal Collection: 27b, 31bl. The Photo Source: 16tl. The Stock Market: 2tl. Tony Stone: 2br, 6l, 12/13b, 20/21t. University College London: 30tl. Werner Forman Archive: 15c.
Every effort has been made to trace the copyright holders and we apologize in advance for any unintentional omissions.
We would be pleased to insert the appropriate acknowledgment in any subsequent edition of this publication.

BARRON'S